The **50**
Best Games for
**Building
Self-Esteem**

The 50 Best Group Games Pocket Books

Example

CONTRACT

A duplicate of this contract is given to: _____ He/she will support me while I honour this contract. At the agreed date, he/she will return the contract and celebrate its completion with me.

_____ (place)

_____ (date)

_____ (signature)
_____ (signature)

Have you seen ...

3 Minute Motivators

More Than 100 Activities to Help you Reach, Teach and Achieve!

Kathy Paterson

This resource will show you how to turn around unmotivated, unfocused classes. With more than 100 practical and simple ideas that will refocus a group, release excess energy, or start a class with a bang.

Offering a wide variety of ready-to-use activities that turn potential problems into opportunities, and get pupils out of a rut and into a more productive mode:

■ *Calm Down* – relaxing activities that let imaginations soar

■ *Get Moving* – lively motivators

■ *Act, Don't Speak* – silent but fun activities

■ *Words and Movement* – activities that mix talk with action

■ *Single Words & Sounds* – simple communication activities

■ *Conversation* – getting motivated one-on-one

■ *Brainstorms* – working together to let the ideas fly

■ *Paper & pencil activities* – from letter and word play to shared stories.

An ideal resource for all teachers, teaching assistants and those running groups, promoting playful activities that involve competition, cooperation and opportunities to focus on real learning.

2008 • 172pp • paperback • 978-1-906531-00-3

Available from

Hinton House Publishers Ltd
Newman House, 4 High Street, Buckingham, MK18 1NT, UK
info@hintonpublishers.com
www.hintonpublishers.com

Self-Commitment

A good way to support the fulfilment of good intentions is a contract that individual group members write and enter into with themselves.

A contract could be worded as follows, for example:

CONTRACT

I _____ agree with myself,
that, by _____ (date) I will
have put the following solution into
action:

_____ (signature)

An additional strategy to ensure that the contract does not just end up in a drawer is to ask a friend or the group leader to countersign the contract.

Working together, the two people who have signed the contract can ensure that it is honoured and, once it has been honoured, can be celebrated together too. An example is given opposite.

Suggestions for solutions

☼ Each person keeps a record of how many times they have put up their hand and how many times they have been picked.

☼ The group leader could deliberately alternate between choosing a boy or a girl.

☼ The group leader no longer chooses individuals to answer, instead, group members select each other. A person who has answered a question chooses the next person, and so on.

Following a group discussion, the group can agree on one of the solutions and try it out. After a time, the effectiveness of the solution can be reviewed and, if necessary, it can be adjusted, or a different solution chosen instead.

Discussion

☼ What kind of experiences are the group having while they work together to solve a given problem?

☼ Did the group realise how strong they could be when they work together as a team?

5 Against 1

Select five people from your group at random. They must then imagine that one member of their group is being approached by five threatening-looking attackers. How can the small group work together, especially as they are at a disadvantage because they are one person down? Give the group five minutes to come up with at least three 'creative' and 'emotionally strong' solutions. In other words, fighting or doing nothing at all are not options!

Such solutions could be:

☼ Shouting 'Fire!' and pointing beyond the attackers.

☼ Coming up with strong points to use in a discussion with the attackers.

☼ Distracting the attackers by all making a loud barking sound.

The group can then use role play to act out the different solutions. Afterwards, choose a new group, who must try to think of further creative solutions to avoid an attack.

This method can also be used to come up with solutions for other problems, including actual problems perceived the group. For example: The boys feel that the group leader seems to prefer the girls. They are asked more often than the boys to answer questions.

Shipwrecked

Ask the group to imagine that they are on a ship which has hit a rock just off a deserted island. The ship has been holed and is sinking slowly, so everyone has to get into the life boat.

In order to make sure that everyone reaches the island on the life boat, only ten items may be taken from the ship. Each item taken must help the group survive once they reach the island.

To start with, each person makes a list of the ten things that they consider to be essential to take with them. Now get the group members to form small groups of up to five people. From their individual lists, the castaways in each group now have to come up with one list of ten items that they all agree on. Depending on the size of your group, continue to merge the smaller groups until everyone is back together again. On each occasion, the lists of items must be cut in order that each group only has ten items on their list at the end of each group phase.

Discussion

☼ Which items did the whole group agree on in the end?

☼ How difficult was it to agree on so few things?

☼ Which criteria were used to select the items?

☼ Is everyone happy with the final list?

To round off the exercise, get the group to practise self-confident body language in pairs. One person demonstrates self-confident body language, the other then copies it. From time to time, reverse the roles until both partners can act self-confidently.

If a camera is available, take a picture of each group members looking confident and print a copy for that person to keep. This can be used, when needed, as a prompt and reassurance that each person *can* act self-confidently.

47

Acting Self-Confidently

There is an association between body language and levels of self-confidence. A person who feels confident generally shows this through their body language. Equally, strength and self-confidence can be gained by deliberately using more confident body language.

Individual group members take turns to stand in front of the group.

☼ How does their body language come across?

☼ Is it self-assured or uncertain?

☼ Natural or affected?

☼ Bored or outgoing?

☼ Which aspects of body language suggest how someone is feeling inside?

Through discussing and trying them out, group members can identify the key features of confident body language, such as:

☼ Standing up straight with the head held high

☼ Maintaining eye contact

☼ Arms hanging down in a relaxed manner

☼ Both feet standing firmly on the floor

☼ Friendly facial expressions

/... continued

Order-Taking

Two group members leave the room. Once outside of the room, they must think of a list of orders that they can give to the other group members, for example, hopping across the room on their left legs, kneeling down in front of them, singing a song, and so on.

The two order-givers come back in again, choose a group member and give the first order. The person being addressed can either accept or reject the order. When rejecting the order, they can do so with or without an explanation. All rejections, even those without an explanation, must be accepted without any further discussion. Following a rejection, the order is simply given to a different group member, who can also choose whether or not to reject it.

Discussion

When all orders have been given, the group discusses how difficult they found it to reject an order. Was it easier to reject an order with or without an explanation?

Stop That!

A role-play exercise to help demonstrate assertiveness and unambiguous communication.

Choose two group members to act out a role play for the rest of the group:

Person A annoys Person B, by pulling B's arm or pushing B around. A continues doing this until B gives an unequivocal signal for A to stop by saying, for example, 'Please stop doing that!'

The group then provides B with feedback about his or her performance. Was B clear enough, should B have behaved more forcefully, was his or her voice loud and strong enough, and so on.

If the pair want to, they can re-enact their performance, taking on board any suggestions that have been made. Alternatively, a different pair can have a go.

Plain-Talking

If people want to be able to assert themselves, they don't just need to be able to communicate unambiguously and clearly in friendly terms, sometimes they also need to be able to communicate a firm rejection.

The group sits in a circle. One after the other, group members turn to their neighbour and succinctly and curtly, but clearly, utter a rejection.

Example

'I don't want to.'
'Leave me alone.'
'Go away.'
'I've had enough.'

These negative utterances can be supported by appropriate gestures, for example, a shaking fist, a pointing finger, and so on.

Evaluation

☼ How difficult was it to act in a negative and unambiguous manner?

☼ Which expressions could be used in real-life situations?

☼ Are some perhaps less appropriate than others?

Yes & No

Saying 'no' can be practised by the whole group at once. This exercise is particularly suitable for groups of younger children.

To start with, divide the group into pairs. Each pair agrees between themselves who is going to say 'No!' and who is going to say 'Yes!'. When told to start, one of each pair begins to continuously say 'Yes!', while the other continuously says 'No!', until everyone is told to 'Stop!'. In the next round, roles are reversed.

Quiet 'No's are not enough. Both 'No!' and 'Yes!' have to be said loudly enough to be heard. If making a lot of noise isn't going to disturb anyone else in the vicinity, encourage the group to shout as loudly as they can.

Which was easier, saying 'Yes' or 'No'?

Note

For some people this sort of exercise may be their first opportunity to dare to oppose a 'Yes' or a 'No' as loudly as possible. Saying 'No' directly and without beating about the bush is very often difficult and sometimes not considered to be appropriate.

Circle of Trust

Ask all of the group members to form a tight circle, standing shoulder to shoulder, facing the middle. Everyone should then stretch their arms out in front of them at chest height. It is very important that everyone stands firmly, with their feet well balanced.

One group member volunteers to stand in the middle, crosses their arms in front of their chest and closes their eyes. When everyone is standing firmly in the circle, the person in the middle – keeping their body straight and strong – lets themselves fall into the hands of the others, forwards, backwards and to the side. The group gently pushes the person in the middle to and fro.

One at a time, group members can take turns to be the person in the middle. However, no-one should be forced to take their turn.

Each group member has to decide the following for themselves:

☼ How much trust do I have in the others?

☼ How much trust do I have in myself, so that I can let myself go?

Discussion

☼ What experiences have I gained during this exercise?

☼ How do I feel now, following the exercise?

Back-to-Back

This simple exercise can be used to demonstrate that, in general, we are stronger when we work together as part of a team.

Divide the group into two subgroups of equal size. Each group forms a long row, standing shoulder to shoulder and linking arms. The two rows should stand opposite each other, facing back-to-back. Draw a chalk line on the floor between the two rows or use an existing line on the floor such as a line in the carpet.

The Game

☼ At a prearranged signal, the two groups should try to push each other across the line. Does one group succeed?

☼ If so, could rearranging the group members within the 'weaker' group give them more strength?

Allow the groups to experiment to discover when they are stronger and when they are weaker.

☼ In which order do group members need to stand in order to make their row as strong as possible?

☼ Is it possible to make both groups equally strong, so that neither manages to push the other across the line?

Journey Into the Future

If a person wants to change, they need to have a vision of how they would like to be.

What are group member's visions of themselves as content and self-confident people?

The following exercise can be used to explore personal visions:

'Imagine yourself in the future. You are ten years older. How do you see yourself now? Write a short report.'

Make sure the written accounts are anonymous.

Exchanging Ideas

Put the reports on the wall in the room so that they can be read by everyone. Discuss the different visions of the future.

☼ What will have to happen to make them become a reality?

☼ What can group members contribute themselves?

☼ What help do they need?

If anyone wants to, they can comment on and explain their own vision of the future.

Standing Up to Group Pressure

Standing up to group pressure requires a significant amount of self-confidence and, for this reason, is not always easy. It's often very hard to admit that one is susceptible to group pressure.

Getting the group to reflect on the problem of group or peer pressure could start, for example, with everyone completing the following task:

Think of a situation where you have been subject to group pressure and have tried not to give in. Describe the situation:

- ☼ What exactly was in that situation that put you under pressure?

- ☼ What did you do to try to not give in to the pressure?

- ☼ Did you succeed in not giving in to the pressure?

- ☼ Were you happy with yourself?

Discussion

Different individual experiences can then be discussed within the group.

- ☼ What is it exactly that creates group pressure?

- ☼ What kind of strategies or behaviours have been useful in helping individuals resist group pressure?

- ☼ Which worked best?

- ☼ Which can be recommended to others?

Code of Honour

This activity helps boys and girls clarify and express how they want to be treated by the opposite sex.

To do this, the group initially divides into groups of girls and boys. Each group holds a discussion and comes up with examples to complete the following sentence: 'We want the boys …' or 'We want the girls …'

For example, the girls could request:

We want the boys to stop making fun of us.
We want the boys to not touch us.

The boys could request, for example:

We want the girls to stop calling us names.
We want the girls not to tell on us.

Discussion

Once both groups have finished their discussions, their requests and wishes are read out and discussed by the whole group.

☼ Are the demands made of the opposite sex acceptable?

☼ Are they already a reality within this group?

☼ Do the demands made by the girls differ significantly from those made by the boys?

☼ How?

Combining the expectations from both groups, a 'code of honour' can be put together: This is how we will treat each other in future!

I-Messages

In order to express a feeling or say something about themselves, people should not use 'you-messages' but instead 'I-messages'.

'You-messages' are messages that start with 'you' and tend to be used to get something across in a round-about way. They can often cause offence or controversy. In contrast, 'I-messages' can express a request or a concern, as well as associated feelings without attacking or hurting the other person.

In everyday communication, we tend to use a lot more you-messages than I-messages. For this reason, it is important to practise formulating I-messages.

Example

Perhaps 'You idiot!' is actually supposed to mean 'I feel really angry with you'.

'You never listen to me!' probably means 'I don't feel you are taking me seriously'.

Divide the group into threes. Two of the group at a time hold a brief conversation about a random, and not particularly demanding topic (for example, 'Where are you planning to go on holiday this year?'). During the conversation, they are only allowed to use I-messages. The third person observes and listens to the conversation and, after it comes to an end, gives feedback about how well the other two did. Then roles are swapped around.

Afterwards, experiences from the small-group work can be discussed by the whole group.

Advertising Campaign

This exercise can be used to demonstrate how to ask for something in a self-confident manner.

Ask the group to invent imaginary products and, for each product, note down the product name and a brief product description on a card. Shuffle the cards and place them face-down. Each person takes a card. Group members can then take it in turns to advertise their chosen product in front of everyone. The rest of the group has to judge the originality and persuasive power of the product description.

Reflection

☼ What does it feel like to stand in front of the group and advertise a product?

☼ What kind of thoughts were going through your mind?

☼ How did your body react?

Negative Notes

Many of the things we don't feel like doing are not actually that bad when it comes down to it. Many fears resolve themselves once we take the time to deal with the things we fear or perceive as too difficult. For some extra help, try the following piece of magic!

During the week, ask the group to write any problem they might encounter on a piece of paper and file them in an envelope or folder. At the end of the week, each person sorts through their file of 'negative notes'.

☼ Which have resolved themselves and can be thrown away?

☼ How many problems have people found a solution for in the meantime?

☼ What is left, what do people need help with?

Discussion

If there are any unresolved problems left over on the 'negative notes', they can be discussed within the group. Working together, group members can look for solutions. Discussion within the group can help provide the support and strength that people need of in order to be brave enough to confront and deal with their problems.

Superwoman & Superman

Identifying with a 'strong' fantasy figure can help to provide self-confidence and emotional strength.

Ask group members think of 'strong' role models from books or films that they would like to emulate. Note the names on the board or a large piece of paper on the wall. Such 'strong' characters could include: Superman, Hermione from Harry Potter, Spiderman, Pippi Longstocking, and so on. Each group member can then choose a hero or heroine and visit them with the help of an imagined journey.

Journey Instructions

'Make yourself comfortable and relax on your chair. … Close your eyes. Imagine you are walking along the road. … At the end of the road there is a statue. … It is a fantastic statue. … On the top stands your hero or heroine … Who is standing on *your* statue? … Can you recognise them clearly? … Your hero or your heroine lifts you up next to them. … He or she puts their hand on your shoulder. … You can feel yourself getting stronger through their touch. … You gain in strength and self-confidence, just like your hero or heroine. … They tell you: I want to share my strength with you. … You will be just like me, brave, self-confident, strong. … If you are ever feeling down, think of me. … I will help you. … Stay on the statue for a little while longer. … You are feeling strong and secure with your hero or heroine. … Now start coming back into the room. Draw a picture of yourself as your hero or heroine.'

Discussion

Afterwards, hang the completed pictures around the room. Group members can talk about why they have chosen a particular figure to identify with. What makes that person so remarkable?

'Walking' the Gauntlet

Group members stand opposite each other in two rows. They take it in turns to individually 'walk' the gauntlet.

This should be done by walking slowly and upright, while looking at the others, smiling all the time, saying 'hello' and not being provoked by any unkind words or gestures.

The people forming the rows have to try to unsettle the person 'walking the gauntlet' by laughing at or teasing them, and using mime and gesture.

Discussion

How difficult was it not be provoked, to remain friendly and not to speed up one's walking pace?

Squeezing Away Negative Feelings

Help your group learn how to squeeze away their negative feelings and worries.

Ask the group members to imagine packing all their negative feelings and thoughts, their worries and fears into a large bag. Now they can screw up the bag and then squeeze it hard with their right hands. They squeeze their hands into a fist, harder and harder, so hard that the negative feelings in the bag become really small. Then they open their fists and simply throw all those compressed negative feelings and thoughts away. Afterwards they can shake their right hands.

If there are still negative feelings and worries left over, the exercise can be repeated using the left hand.

The Story of My Name

Each name has a story. Often, parents give their children names that they associate with a person they like, with something positive, and with good feelings to help set their children up for a successful life.

Discussion

Group members reflect on the story behind and the meaning of their own names.

☀ What does their name mean?

☀ Can they think of a 'strong' or successful person who has the same name?

☀ What kind of strength can they gain from this for themselves?

My Personal Coat of Arms

Special skills and strengths can be represented using objects, animals, symbols and so on. To start with, get the group to come up with and collect ideas for such images.

Example

☼ A lion could stand for a special strength

☼ Two hands touching each other for helpfulness

☼ A sword for courage

☼ A horse for speed.

You may even have a group member whose family actually has a personal coat of arms and who can explain the imagery to the rest of the group.

Give all group members a sheet of paper with the outline of a coat of arms. Ask them to create and draw their own personal coat of arms using symbols and pictures that say something about their individual strengths and abilities.

Completed coats of arms can be exhibited and discussed by the whole group. What do the coats of arms say about the skills of the individual group members?

Personal Ad

Ask each group member to write their own personal advert. The advert should promote the individual and emphasise their special skills, positive characteristics and behaviour patterns.

Once all adverts have been completed, set up a 'market', where everyone has to present and defend their personal ad, providing further information in response to enquiries, and generally promoting themselves. Group members are allowed to embellish and expand on whatever they have said in their adverts, but must stay within the realms of truth.

Discussion

☼ What kind of experiences did people have while putting together their personal ads?

☼ How did they get on at the market?

I Like Being a Girl – I Like Being a Boy

Divide the group into small groups of girls and boys.

On a poster-size piece of paper, the girl's group must try to write down as many statements as possible to complete the sentence: 'I like being a girl, because …';

The boy's group does the same for: 'I like being a boy, because …'.

Discussion

Afterwards, discuss the posters within the whole group.

☼ What kind of reasons are given by the girls, and what kind of reasons by the boys?

☼ How much do the statements differ?

☼ Are there differences between girls and boys?

☼ What are they?

The Hot Seat

This is quite a well-known exercise. The group sits in a circle. One group member sits on a chair in the middle and then moves the 'hot seat' from one person to the next.

Each group member they stop in front of has to tell the person in the hot seat something that they rate about him or her. The person in the hot seat is not allowed to comment but has to quietly 'endure' the compliments.

Discussion

Once everyone has had turn, discuss the experience within the group.

☼ How difficult is it to be praised?

☼ What is it like having to say something positive about someone you may not know very well?

What I Like About Myself

Most people are not used to, or feel awkward about, discussing their own strengths. It is even more difficult to do this in front of others.

In order to practise appropriate self-praise, ask group members to select a partner who they feel they can trust and be open with. They then take turns to talk for three minutes explaining what they like about themselves.

Discussion

Talk about this activity within the whole group. How did group members feel while they were talking and while they were listening?

A useful group activity is to discuss and work out the differences between 'valuing oneself' and 'boasting'.

26

These symbols of strength could be, for example, a lion, a bright rising sun, and so on.

Afterwards, give group members the opportunity to talk about the experiences they had on their journey.

Extension

Encourage individuals in the group to remember the phrase, image or colours that they found for their own feeling of strength and to try to recall this when they are in need of strength.

Journey to Your Own Strengths

A great way to think about one's own strengths is to go on an imaginary journey. Ask the group members to settle in a relaxed and comfortable position, then the journey can start. You can change the wording and content as necessary according to the age and needs of your group members.

The Imaginary journey

'Close your eyes. ... Let your thoughts go back in time by a few weeks ... months ... years ... in your life .... Go back to situations where you felt happy ... strong ... self-confident ... able .... Choose a situation where you felt particularly great. ...

What did you see? ... What kind of images? ... What colours? ... What could you hear? ... Which voices were particularly pleasing? ... What was your voice like? ... What kind of smells do you remember? ... What could you feel? ... What did you do that made you feel so great? ... What was it that gave you such a strong feeling of wellbeing and strength? ...

Try to come up with a word or sentence that describes this strength. ... Have you thought of something appropriate? ...

Now take three deep breaths ... stretch your whole body ... and come back to the group and open your eyes. Now write down the word or sentence that you came up with for your strength. Or you could draw a picture. Use colours that match your strength ...'

Elevenses

Personal strengths can be described particularly well in poem form using 'Elevenses'. 'Elevenses' are poems that consist of 11 words distributed across five lines as follows:

Line 1: one word
Line 2: two words
Line 3: three words
Line 4: four words
Line 5: one word

Example

William
A boy
He is strong
And proud and self-confident
Really!

Selina
A girl
Clever and sympathetic
Knows what she wants
Honestly!

Discussion

Using this format, group members might reveal something about themselves that they might usually find hard to say.

☼ Did they actually do this?

☼ Was it easy or difficult to come up with a positive self-portrait?

My Name – My Programme

The individual letters of people's names can be used to highlight or to wish for 'strong' characteristics or abilities in oneself. Group members can either use their own names or choose someone else to describe.

Example

Sweet
Happy
Artistic
Realistic
Outgoing
Nimble

Jolly
Approachable
Self-assured
Optimistic
Noble

A bit more tricky, but just as much fun, is for players to come up with a whole sentence for their first names. For example:

Sharon
Has
A
Really
Outgoing
Nature.

Just
A
S weet
Old-fashioned
Nobleman.

Discussion

The personal descriptions or sentences can be put on the wall or read aloud. People's views of themselves or others can be discussed by the group and commented on.

☼ Do the associations really apply to the actual person?

☼ Or was it just about finding words that started with a given letter?

I am – I can – I have

Write the following three sentence starters on cards or sheets of paper, one for each person, and stick one sheet to each group members' back:

☼ I am…

☼ I can…

☼ I have…

Everyone now takes a pen and walks around the room. While doing so, each person has to complete one of the sentences on someone's back using a 'strong' comment. These comments should be relevant to the individual person. The game ends once all sentences have been completed. Everyone then takes off their card and reads what sort of strengths others in the group have attributed to them.

Discussion

☼ How did the group members feel during this game?

☼ How do they feel now they have read the card?

☼ Are they surprised about the attributes on the card or would they have appraised themselves in the same way?

Note

Writers should remain anonymous during this game. This way it is easier for group members to say something positive about someone even though they might not dare to say it out loud.

I Am Strong Stephanie

Group members sit in a circle and take turns introducing their strengths to the rest of the group. They must state their name and one of their 'strong' attributes:

Example

☼ 'I am helpful Kathy.'

☼ 'I am fast John.'

Variations

The game can be made more difficult by players having to repeat all the previous introductions before they can say their own name, for example:

'That is helpful Kathy, that is fast John and I am happy Tim.'

An additional level of difficulty can be introduced by having the 'strong' attribute begin with the same letter as player's name:

'That is kind Kathy, that is jolly John, that is truthful Tim and I am strong Stephanie.'

Balance

Group members get together in pairs. The aim of the game is to remain in balance with one's partner while carrying out different activities.

Example

☼ Stand opposite each other and hold hands. Pull each other to and fro, but make sure you maintain your position without moving your feet.

☼ Stand on one leg and pull to and fro while keeping your balance.

☼ Stand back to back with backs in contact. Squat down together and then stand up again, keeping contact all the time.

☼ Place your hands on each others shoulders, close your eyes and sway to the right and then to the left.

After a few exercises, players should change partners.

Discussion

☼ Is it easy or difficult to 'maintain balance' with another person?

☼ Does it vary for each partner?

☼ What did people find out about others during this exercise?

☼ What did they find out about themselves?

Reflecting

Group members sit opposite each other in pairs. One of them makes some movements and their partner has to copy them to form a mirror image.

The game can then be extended. Different activities can be demonstrated, for example, painting a picture, assembling a simple object, and so on, which the 'mirror image' partner has to follow.

After a little while, the roles can be reversed.

19

Talking Hands

Group members sit opposite each other in pairs. They close their eyes and then try to 'talk' to each other through touch by using only their hands.

Discussion

☼ What did they talk about?

☼ How did they feel while they were 'talking'?

☼ How often were they tempted to use their voices to aid communication and also to open their eyes?

Variation

This exercise is easier if a topic of conversation is decided upon beforehand, which can then be discussed using only hands. The group could be given the instruction to discuss the same topic in an 'agitated and angry manner' and then again in a 'confident and calm manner'.

Stroking Hedgehogs

Group members get together in pairs.

One partner in each pair becomes the hedgehog. They curl up into a ball on the floor like a hedgehog (pulling their knees in, closing their eyes, putting their heads onto their knees and wrapping their arms around their knees) and try to imagine that they feel hurt and offended. Their partner has to try to get them out of this state of isolation. In order to do so, they can stroke the 'hedgehog', talk to it, gently roll it backwards and forwards and so on. Afterwards, the pairs reverse roles.

Group members must not use force to unroll the 'ball'. In addition, be aware that some group members may feel uncomfortable with being stroked and touched and allow anyone to sit this activity out if they wish.

Discussion

At the end of this activity give the group the opportunity to talk about their experiences in the different roles.

☼ What worked best for different individuals to relax the 'tense' hedgehogs?

☼ Were there any personal resistances or any very personal aids?

4 Something that only one group member likes

Example

☀ Classical music

☀ Getting up early

☀ Household chores

Discussion

Bring the group back together to discuss the answers.

☀ How difficult was it to find commonalities and differences?

☀ Is there anything within the group as a whole that really only one person likes or dislikes?

☀ Did group members learn anything about the others that they did not previously know or would never have suspected?

Threesomes

Divide the group into threes. If necessary, you can also have one or two groups of four. If so, adjust the game instructions accordingly.

Each group has to complete the following tasks. They have to list on sheets of paper:

1 Three things that all three group members do not like

Example

☀ Injustice

☀ When it rains during the holidays

☀ Tidying up their rooms

2 Three things all of them do like

Example

☀ Holidays

☀ Swimming

☀ Good marks

3 Something that only one group member does not like

Example

☀ Mental arithmetic

☀ Visiting relatives

☀ Spinach

Feminine – Masculine

The group sits in a circle. Pairs of boys and girls are selected at random. In turn, one pair of boys and then girls is called into the middle of the circle. Each pair is given instructions to carry out the same activity or role play.

Example

☼ Arguing with each other

☼ Being affectionate with each other

☼ Being cross with each other

☼ Comforting each other

Discussion

☼ Do boys and girls express their feelings differently?

☼ What are the differences?

Afterwards, reverse the roles - now the girls must try to behave like the boys and vice versa.

☼ How did the girls and boys feel during this role reversal?

Animal Brilliance

Each group member imagines they are an animal. Ask them to write the name of their animal on a piece of paper along with a short explanation of why they have chosen that particular one. They should also write their own name on the piece of paper before folding and placing it in a box or bag.

Then, as a whole, the group agrees on an animal for each individual and these animals are compared with the animals that each group member chose for themselves as the descriptions are selected and read out.

Discussion

☼ Did the group and the individuals agree on the same animal?

☼ Did they at least name an animal close to the one chosen by the individual?

☼ For which group members were there discrepancies and why?

Instead of animals, you can vary this exercise by using plants, vehicles, a piece of furniture, a musical instrument and so on.

Experiencing self and others through metaphor is generally less stressful than direct feedback. In addition, metaphors tend to contain positive as well as negative feedback.

Wish List

Ask each group member to write on a piece of paper the answers to various questions about likes and dislikes, for later discussion.

Example

☼ What kind of music do you like to listen to?

☼ Which famous person would you most like to meet?

☼ What sort of characteristics would someone have to have for you to want to be friends with them?

Discussion

The pieces of paper are then shuffled and redistributed, and the group must work together to try to work out who has written on which piece of paper. In order for the task not to become too unwieldy, large groups can be split into smaller ones at the beginning of the activity.

While allocating and discussing the 'wish lists', group members have to start talking to each other and will get to know each other better. This is a good activity to use as an ice-breaker.

Soul Mates

For this activity you will need a bag. Ask each group member to bring to the group a small item that they feel represents themselves.

Each group member places their small personal item into a bag, without anybody else looking. One by one, each person draws an item from the bag, again without looking.

As a whole, the group must think about who a particular item might belong to. More than one person can be named, but each suggestion must be justified.

Discussion

☀ Did the group identify the real owners of the different items?

☀ Do the group members who were linked to an item have anything in common with the actual owner of the item?

☀ Did they realise this before?

Personality Profiles

For this game, you will need large rolls of paper and pens. Use the paper to draw the silhouette outline of each group member.

These outlines can then be brought to life. For each group member get everyone to record that individual's characteristics, behaviours, their skills, favourite activities, peculiarities, etc, on their outline. Each group member is allowed to write something in everybody else's outline but, of course, insults are not allowed.

Discussion

Afterwards, discuss the different personality profiles within the group.

- ☼ Do group members recognise themselves?

- ☼ Do they see themselves the same way as others do or do they think they are completely different?

- ☼ Have they learned anything new about themselves or others?

Self-Esteem Paradox

Ask group members to think of examples of behaviours that they would not consider to be particularly self-confident. Write these on the board or a large sheet of paper.

Examples

☼ blushing

☼ running away

☼ making excuses

Discussion

☼ Have group members experienced any of the behaviours themselves?

☼ In what kind of situations?

☼ How did they feel at the time?

☼ If these behaviours are not considered to be 'self-confident', what sort of behaviours would be 'self-confident'?

Self-Esteem – What Does It Mean?

Divide into smaller groups of three or four people. Ask the smaller groups to use role play to portray situations of everyday conflict for the rest of the group. Role-play situations can be brainstormed and written on cards for selection.

Examples

☼ A teenager wants more pocket money. However, their family does not have much money to spare.

☼ Members of a gang are trying to persuade a new member, who dislikes smoking, to smoke a cigarette.

Try to play each situation through several times, each time with a different ending. On each occasion, the audience has to decide whether the players have behaved assertively. Each decision has to be justified. If the audience feels that a role play did not include any assertive or self-confident behaviour, they should make further suggestions for developing the role play.

Strong Interviews

Opinions from outside, as well as inside a group, can enrich a group's discussions.

Ask group members to form pairs, take a note pad and, where available, a means of recording and go outside the room to ask people they meet the following questions:

☼ 'What does human strength mean to you?'

☼ 'In order for you to consider a woman or a man as strong, what would they have to be like?'

Anybody who works in the building can be asked, for example, teachers, other group leaders, the caretaker, office staff, cleaners, kitchen personnel, visitors and so on.

Discussion

Afterwards, analyse the interviews within the group.

☼ What definitions of strength have been given by different people?

☼ Are there different opinions amongst different professional groups?

☼ Are there differences with regard to the opinions of women and men?

☼ Have the group members come across new viewpoints which they had not previously considered?

Strong Women & Men

Ideas of what makes a strong woman or a strong man can vary considerably. Working independently, ask group members to think of five ideas each to complete the following sentences:

Women are strong when ...
Men are strong when ...

Discussion

Collate the individual contributions and compare the different images of strong women and men.

☼ What is considered to be a female strength?

☼ What is male strength?

☼ Are there different perceptions with regard to female and male strengths between the genders in the group?

☼ Why are there differences?

☼ How does the group justify them?

☼ Are the reasons given justified?

Strong Body Language

Ask everyone to write down a 'strong' feeling (e.g., happiness, contentment) or a 'strong' behaviour (helping others, showing courage) on a piece of paper.

Fold the pieces of paper and collect them in a box. Group members can then take it in turns to choose a piece of paper and express the feeling or behaviour by using mime, gesture or movement. The rest of the group has to guess what is being mimed.

Discussion

☼ What was easy to portray, what was difficult?

☼ What was easy to guess, what was more difficult?

☼ How does it feel to express 'strong' feelings or behaviours, when maybe you are not used to feeling particularly strong yourself?

☼ Does 'strong' body language make a person feel strong?

Strong Sayings

The topic of emotional strength and self-esteem doesn't have to be serious. On the contrary, introducing fun and humour can facilitate discussions about human strengths and weaknesses.

First, ask the group to collect sayings or lines from songs and poems, especially nonsense or humorous ones, about strengths and also about weaknesses, such as:

When all else fails, read the directions.
Happiness can't buy money.

Then ask the group to have a go at coming up with their own strong sayings, for example:

I'd rather be in strong arms than on weak legs.
This country needs strong women.

Variation

'Strong Sayings' can also be played as a competition.

Split the group into several small groups consisting of three or four people. Each small group makes up their own sayings and then agree on the best and most original one. Now each group presents their saying to the group as a whole.

Points can then be awarded using a secret voting system. Each group member is allowed to award five points. The points can all be allocated to one saying or they can be distributed between a number of sayings. However, points must not be given to their own group's saying.

The saying with the most points wins. Discuss why this saying was chosen.

Three Strong Corners

Posters with the following statements are put up in three corners of the room:

1 A person who is strong will never become weak.
2 A person who is strong does not show any weaknesses.
3 A person who is strong can admit their weaknesses.

Ask the group members to decide which statement best represents their personal opinion. Each person should then go to the corner corresponding to their statement and talk to the people in that group for a few minutes, trying to find reasons and examples to support 'their' argument.

Each group must then decide on a spokesperson who will represent their statement in a whole-group discussion.

Discussion

☼ How did the discussion go?

☼ What kinds of reasons were given to support the different statements?

☼ Did one argument win and get accepted by everyone?

☼ Which one?

☼ Why?

Word Chains

For this game, you will need index cards or pieces or strips of paper.

The group members make up word chains – where each word must start with the last letter of the previous word – using words that, in their opinion, are associated with strength.

Example

courage – eagle – education – nobleman - …

As well as saying the words aloud each group member must write down their word and one after the other these can be stuck to the board or wall. The game ends when no one can think of another connecting word.

Reflection

Following the end of the game, use the words to reflect on the term 'strength'. How do different group members perceive or define strength?

Feeling Strong is Like ...

A good way to get group members to think about self-esteem or emotional strength is to ask them to think of metaphors to complete the sentence starting 'Feeling strong is like ...'.

Write the first part of the sentence in large letters on pieces of flipchart paper, which can be stuck to the wall. Group members can write their metaphors on strips of paper or card and then stick or pin them to the sheets on the wall.

Example

Feeling strong is like

☼ ... *biting into a freshly baked piece of buttered bread.*

☼ ... looking down onto cars from the steering wheel of a truck.

☼ ... being tanned and riding the waves.

Discussion

☼ What kind of wishes, needs and fantasies about feeling strong are highlighted through these metaphors?

☼ Is 'feeling strong' the same as 'feeling superior'?

☼ Is it possible to feel strong inside without dominating others?

The ABC of Emotional Strength

Brainstorm ideas about the topic 'emotional strength' by preparing sheets of paper listing the letters of the alphabet. Give every person their own piece of paper and ask them to write down a 'strong' word, a 'strong' sentence or a 'strong' idea for each letter.

Examples

A	Active	N	Never never land
B	Brilliant bloke	O	Over the moon
C	Content	P	Protest
D	Deft	Q	Quick thinking
E	Easily the best	R	Reaching for the stars
F	Friendship	S	Successful
G	Great Minds	T	Talent
H	Having hundreds of pounds	U	Unbelievably clever
I	Intelligence	V	Very powerful
J	Jackpot	W	Wealthy
K	Kung Fu	X	Xmas
L	Laugh a lot	Y	Young forever
M	Magic moments	Z	Zany

Evaluation & Discussion

Individual results for each letter can then be collated on the board or a large piece of paper. This way, the group can create a wealth of terms and ideas which describe 'being emotionally strong' and which can introduce the group to the topic by providing a platform for discussion.

'Playing is not idleness, but the highest form of energy.'

– *Peter Lippert*

Contents

Contents

Published by

Hinton House Publishers Ltd
Newman House, 4 High Street, Buckingham, MK18 1NT, UK

info@hintonpublishers.com
www.hintonpublishers.com

First published 2008
Reprinted 2009, 2010, 2011, 2012, 2013, 2014

Printed in the United Kingdom by Hobbs the Printers Ltd

British Library Cataloguing in Publication Data
Portmann, Rosemarie
  The 50 best games for building self-esteem. – (The 50 best group games pocket books ; v. 1)
  1. Self-esteem 2. Group games
  I. Title II. Building self-esteem III. The fifty best games for building self-esteem
  158.1

ISBN-13: 9781906531188

Originally published in German by Don Bosco
Verlag München under the title *Die 50 besten
Spiele fürs Selbstbewusstsein*
© Don Bosco Verlag, München 2005

The **50**
Best Games for
Building
Self-Esteem

Rosemarie Portmann
translated by Lilo Seelos

HINTON**HOUSE**